First edition October, 2022.

ISBN: 979-8-218-07324-4

SparkBrightKids.com

FOR GROWNUPS

Thank you for your commitment to raising kind kids! It's a small step we can all take to make the world a better place.

The Kindness Workbook for Kids was written to be successful with a range of ages, but was specifically written with elementary school children in mind. That said, the activities and prompts allow kids to respond at their current development and academic level. Younger children may benefit from a grownup reading aloud and supporting them with the activities, and older kids may want to take things further.

This book explores kindness through five levels: kind to myself, kind to my family, kind to my community, kind to my peers, and kind to my planet. You know your child best, and probably have an idea of which levels will come easily and which may take more work. You can explore the book in any order, and do not need to complete all the activities.

The Kindness Workbook for Kids employs two frameworks. First, we believe that kindness is not an innate trait, but a skill that can be taught and a habit that can be formed. Fostering this belief in kids helps them develop a growth mindset. Remember that there are many ways children learn and acquire new skills. This book will give them hands on practice in making kind choices, but be sure you model kindness throughout the five levels as well.

The next framework is called metacognition, or thinking about our own thinking. Throughout the book, kids will think through which choices they make and why they make them. Metacognition is a powerful tool for developing self-awareness and helping kids realize they are in control of their own thoughts and choices. Check out the journal and tracker sections of this book to help your child connect its content to their real life experience.

Above all, have fun making the world a kinder place!

CONTENTS

Plus Kindness Journal & Trackers!

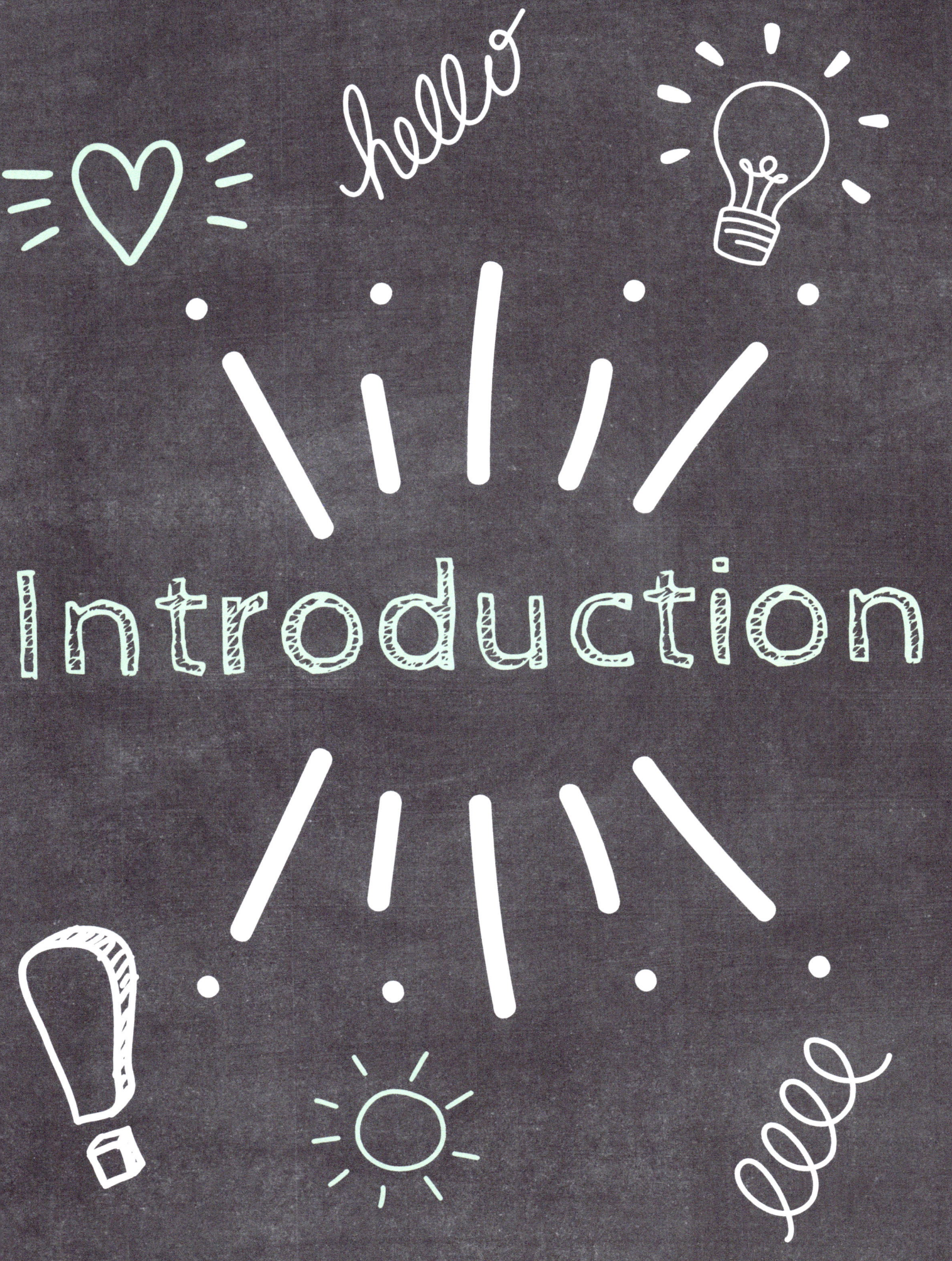

What is Kindness?

What is kindness anyway? Kindness is a choice. Kindness is choosing to do something that makes a positive impact for someone or something. Kindness can be big or small, and kindness can become a habit. Like any habit, you can learn it by practicing it. This workbook will help you do just that! Imagine: what could the world be like if people chose kindness every day?

It's also important to remember what kindness isn't. The world's problems or other people's troubles are not your responsibility to fix. Sure, you can make a difference by choosing kindness and inspiring others to do the same, but you can't control other people's choices or circumstances. Choosing kindness also doesn't mean that you need to feel happy or positive all the time. That wouldn't be healthy! It is normal and healthy to experience the full range of emotions. And finally, if you're kind to someone and they are unkind back to you, you don't have to keep trying. If you ever feel uncomfortable, tell a trusted grownup.

Remember, you can't control other people's choices, but you can control your own. So, let's make kindness a simple choice that can make a big difference!

How to Use this Book

This book is made to be used however you want! You don't have to read or complete every page, and you don't have to go through it in order from beginning to end (although you can if you want to)! Flip through it, see which sections or ideas seem most exciting to you and start there. You can doodle in the margins, scribble notes inside the cover, and dog-ear the pages.

The back of the book includes a week's worth of daily journal pages and month's worth of weekly tracker pages. If you want to keep going, use a notebook and follow the prompts. There is also a year's worth of monthly tracker pages so you can keep track of your progress long-term. You might want to use all of these sections or just one—whatever you like best!

Where do I Start?

There are so many opportunities to be kind every day that you might be wondering where to start! Remember, kindness is a choice, and you can choose to be kind in all kinds of ways. This book is organized by five Levels of Kindness: being kind to yourself, your family, your peers, your community, and your planet. Check out the diagram on the next page—here's how it works:

1 To truly make kindness a habit, you must remember to be kind to yourself. How you treat your mind, body, and heart has a big impact on how you feel. People who are kind to themselves can spread kindness more easily to others—that's why you are at the center of the Levels of Kindness.

2 The next level is all about family. Families come in all shapes and sizes, and no matter how yours looks, your family are probably the people you spend the most time with. Being kind to your family has a big impact on the people you love most and can contribute to harmony and fun at home.

3 School, sports, clubs, camps, these are the places where you encounter your peers —other kids around your age and our next Level of Kindness. Your peers can include your friends, kids you don't know that well yet, and even kids you might not always get along with. Spreading kindness among your peers can make a big impact on someone's life!

4 Think about all the places and spaces in your community, our next Level of Kindness. From parks and libraries, to stores and fire stations, the place you live and learn will always benefit from a little more kindness.

5 And finally, our last Level of Kindness is home-sweet-home—your planet. The Earth supports all life, from tiny microorganisms, to gigantic whales, to you yourself. Everything on Earth is interdependent and kindness toward our planet will ring out in big ways.

Levels of Kindness

Your Planet

Your Community

Your Peers

Your Family

You!

How Does Kindness Make Me Feel?

Think about a time someone was kind to you, and answer these questions:

1. In which Level of Kindness did it occur?

_____

2. How did it impact your day?

_____

3. Write or draw the emotions you felt in the yellow notepad.

Think about a time you were kind, and answer these questions:

1. In which Level of Kindness did it occur?

_____

2. How did it impact your day?

_____

3. Write or draw the emotions you felt in the purple notepad.

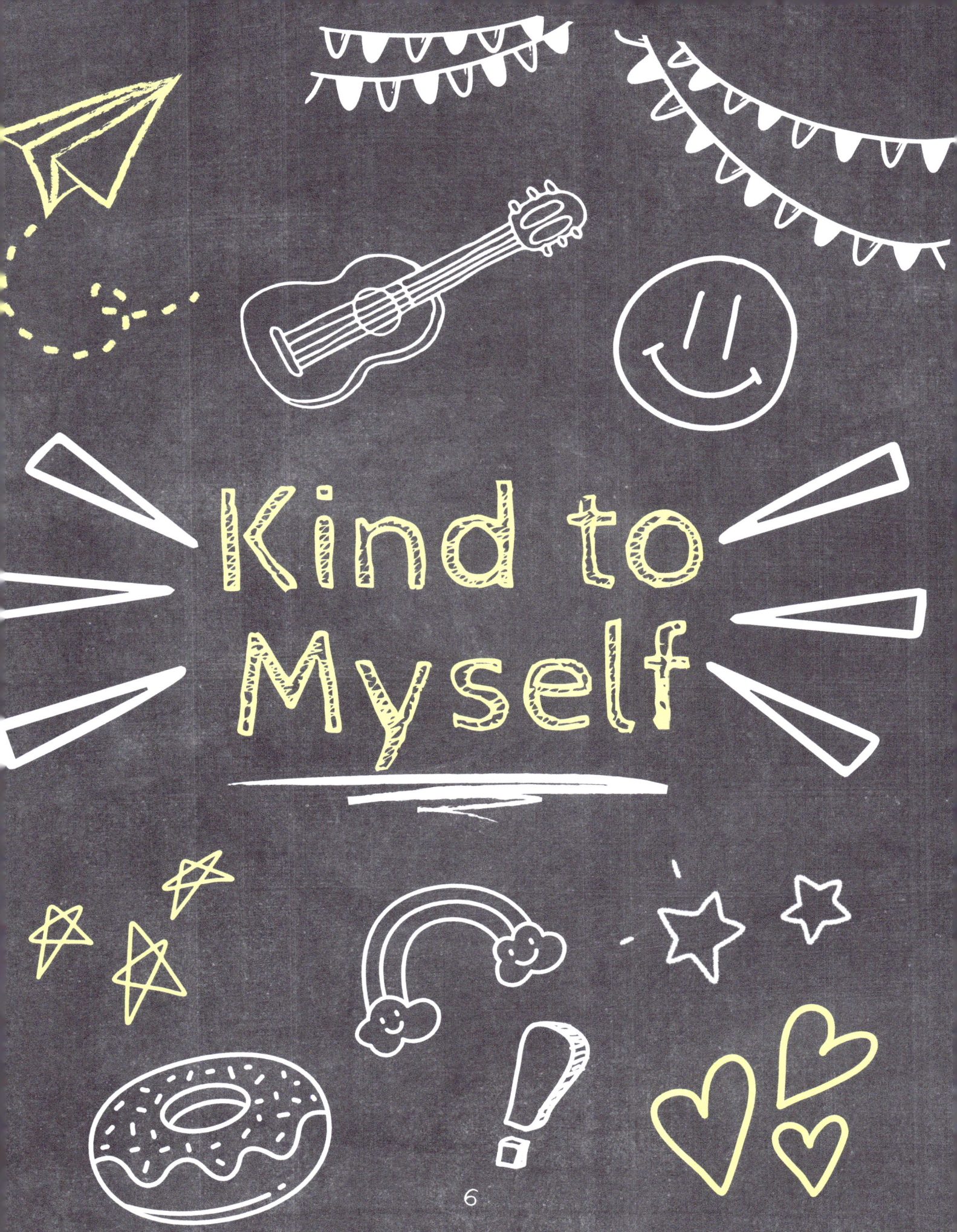

Kind to Myself

Ways to Be Kind to Myself

It's hard to be kind to others if you aren't kind to yourself. Let's explore the many ways you can practice self-kindness!

1 Be kind to your body.

✓ Eat a healthy, balanced diet.
✓ Exercise and stay active.
✓ Get plenty of sleep.

2 Be kind to your mind.

✓ Develop a growth mindset.
✓ Stretch your creativity.
✓ Practice mindfulness.

3 Be kind to your heart.

✓ Practice gratitude.
✓ Celebrate yourself.
✓ Develop healthy self-talk.

Complete the green notepad!

About Me

Name:

Age:

Favorite way to stay active:

Something I'm excited to learn one day:

What I love about being me:

⊦⊢ Kind to My Body ⊦⊢

Being kind to your body can have a big impact on your mood and thoughts. Complete these activities to make an action plan!

Plan Your Plate!

First, draw what your typical dinner plate looks like now.

Next, draw a nutritious, well-balanced dinner including vegetables, fruit, grains, and protein.

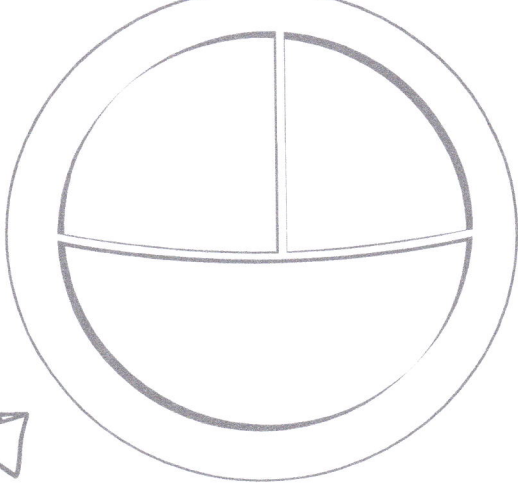

Finally, draw your typical dinner plate again, but make at least one change. Swap something from your first drawing with something from your second drawing to make a small improvement.

Try a change like this at one or two meals this week—every little choice can mean big kindness toward your body!

Activity Planner

Staying active does more than make us strong—it also impacts our mental health. Most kids need about an hour of exercise every day, but it doesn't have to happen all at once. One of the great things about being a kid is that there are plenty of opportunities to be active each day. Complete the planner below to make exercise a habit of self-kindness.

Write or draw how you plan to stay active every day of the week!

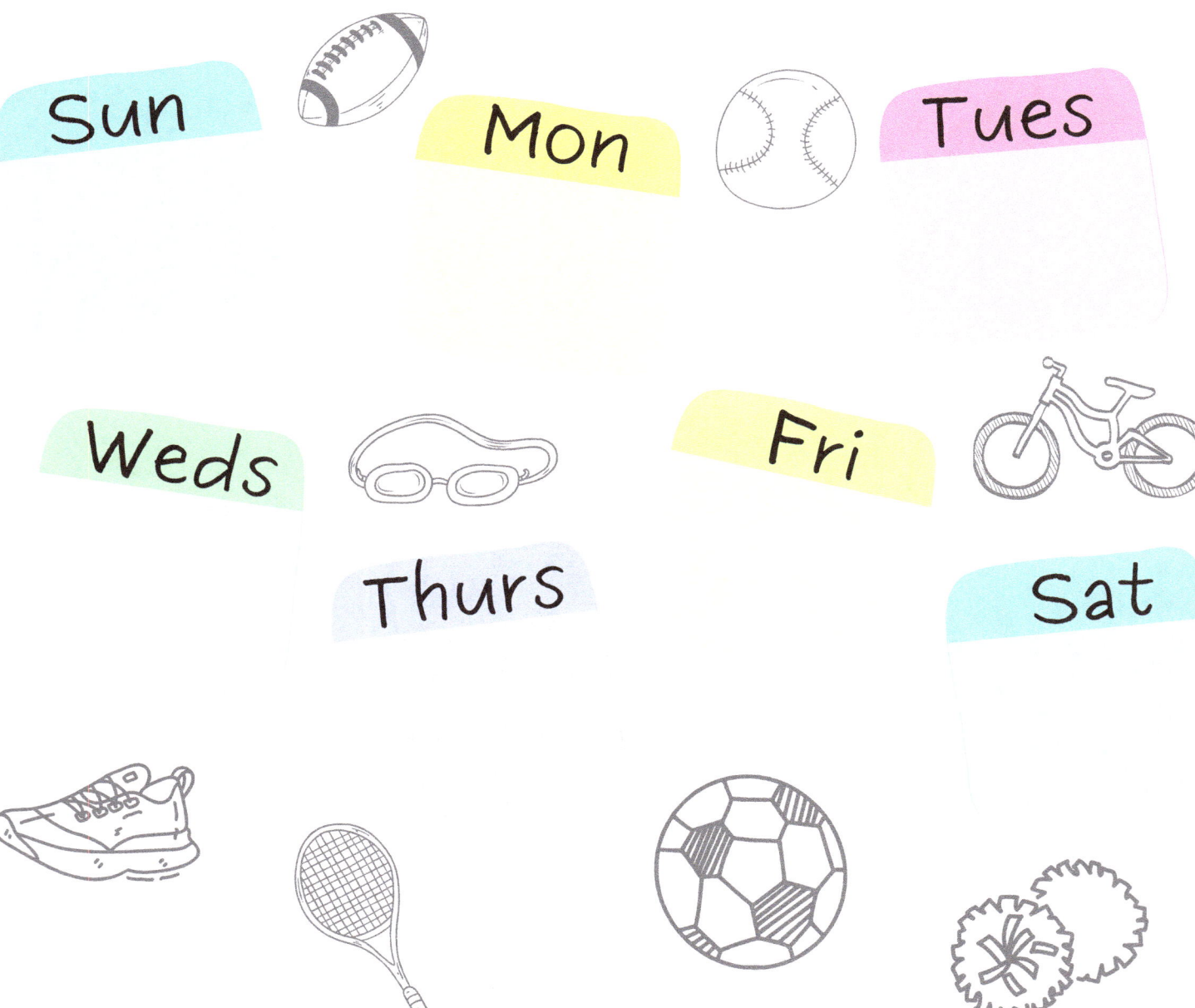

Sleep Planner

It can be so tempting to stay up late to watch a show, read a book, play a video game, or chat with friends. But the quality and quantity of our sleep has a big effect on our overall health and mood. When you get enough sleep, you are better able to pay attention and learn. What's more, both your mental and physical health improve!

What time do you go to bed now? _____

What time do you wake up now? _____

How many hours of sleep is that? _____

Now, look at the recommended hours of sleep per-night by age in the chart. Are you getting enough sleep? If so, keep up the great work! If not, write a new bedtime and wake-up time in the alarm clocks below.

Lights Out!

Rise & Shine!

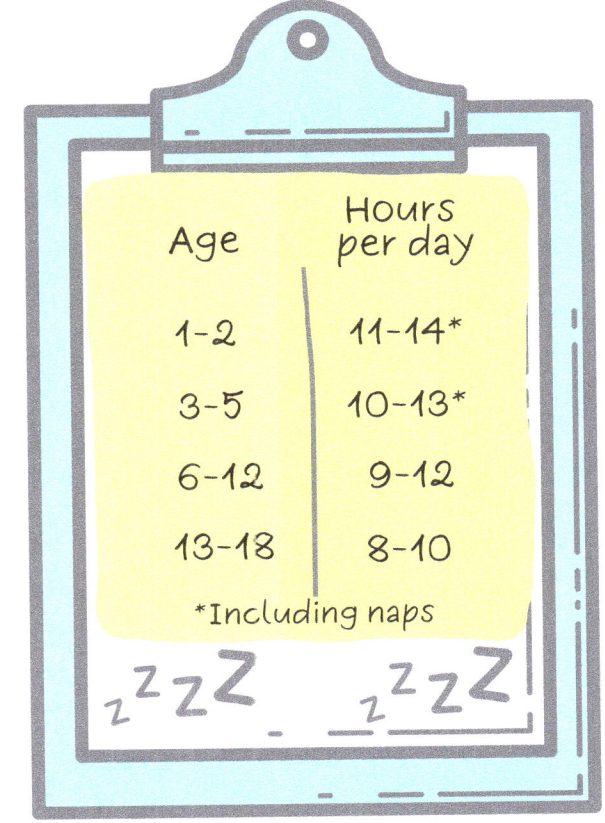

Age	Hours per day
1-2	11-14*
3-5	10-13*
6-12	9-12
13-18	8-10

*Including naps

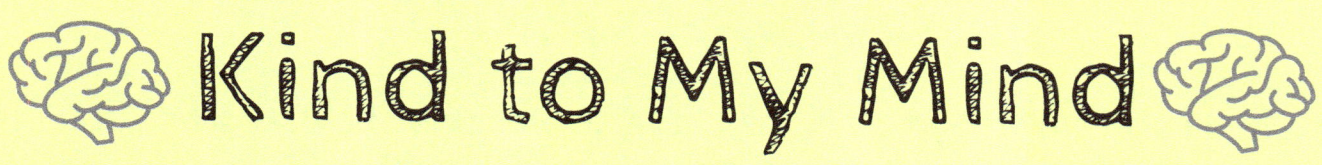

Kind to My Mind

It is as important to be kind to your mind as it is to your body. Complete these activities to build a habit of mental kindness.

Develop a Growth Mindset

One way to be kind to your mind is to develop a growth mindset. Someone with a growth mindset believes that their abilities can be improved through things like practice and effort. Someone with a fixed mindset, on the other hand, believes that they are either good at something or not, and there is nothing they can do to change it. This book was made with a growth mindset in mind. Everyone can become kinder by practicing kindness!

Change these fixed mindset statements into growth mindset statements.

Fixed Mindset	Growth Mindset
I won first place because I am an excellent athlete.	I won first place because I practiced every day and my hard work is helping me become an excellent athlete.
I am not good at math.	Math doesn't come easily to me, but when I put in the effort to learn it I get better at it every day.
I'm great at piano because I'm talented.	
I am not creative.	_____
He got an A because he's smart.	_____
She's better at soccer than I am.	_____

Foster Creativity

Creativity is one of the things that make us human. And just like kindness, everyone can be creative! Being creative simply means putting your imagination to use, and it's kind to your mind to stretch it in new ways. Try some of these activities to get those creative juices flowing.

Show-in-a-Box

Find a box and walk around your home collecting the following items: something blue, something fuzzy, something smooth, something funny, and something to wear. Next, write a scene that incorporates all these items. Finally, gather some others and act it out!

Paint-a-Scene

Draw or paint a place that you know well-- this could be a room or a favorite outdoor location. Next, draw it again, but this time add a magic "what if?" What if aliens landed there? What if a family of purple pigs came to visit? Come up with your own "what if?" and have fun!

Poet-Tree

Imagine that your favorite tree could think or talk. Write four poems from the perspective of the tree, one for each season of the year. Think about what the tree might think or feel with each new season.

Set a timer for two minutes and see how many uses for a tire you can come up with. Let yourself think outside the box!

Practice Mindfulness

There can be a lot of stressful things in the world, and sometimes it can feel overwhelming. Mindfulness is the practice of focusing on the present moment, and it's a great way to be kind to your mind. Mindfulness can help you control your behavior and become aware of your thoughts and feelings. These are important skills when building the habit of kindness. Try these activities to develop a practice of mindfulness.

Make a Mindfulness Jar

Add three types of glitter to an empty plastic bottle or jar (try different colors and sizes). Add a big spoonful of glitter glue to the bottle and fill it up with water. If you want to, add a couple of drops of food coloring. Stir the mixture thoroughly. One type of glitter represents your thoughts, one type represents your feelings, and the third type represents your actions. When you shake the bottle, the glitter swirls together just as our thoughts, feelings, and actions do throughout the day. Put the jar down and breath deeply as you watch the glitter settle to the bottom. Notice how the thoughts, feelings, and actions settle. Shake the bottle and watch it settle anytime you need a mindfulness moment.

Five Senses Meditation

Meditation is an activity that helps us focus our minds on the present moment. It's a great tool for building a habit of mindfulness! Try this meditation whenever you need some calm and focus.

Take a deep breath in and slowly let it out.
    Silently notice 5 things that you can see.
    Silently notice 4 things that you can feel.
    Silently notice 3 things that you can hear.
    Silently notice 2 things that you can smell.
    Silently notice 1 thing that you can taste.

End with another deep breath in and out.

♥ Kind to My Heart ♥

We've explored ways to be kind to your body and mind, but what about your emotions? Being kind to your heart means treating yourself kindly and compassionately.

Develop an Attitude of Gratitude

Gratitude means being thankful for something or someone, and it can have a big effect on your mood and outlook. When you are grateful, you appreciate the good things in your life and your brain gets the signal to boost your mood—talk about being kind to your heart! Try some of these activities to cultivate an attitude of gratitude.

Gratitude Tree

Make a gratitude tree! Draw a tree with branches—but no leaves—on a large piece of paper. Next, cut out leaf shapes from colorful construction paper. Cut out as many as you'd like for your tree. Write something you are thankful for on each leaf and glue it onto your tree. When you are done, you will have a beautiful poster reminding you of everything you are grateful for!

Just Because Notes

We all know it's polite to send a thank you note when someone gives you a present, but think about how someone would feel if you gave them a note just because you were grateful for something they said or did. Write a note to someone thanking them for something you are grateful for, and watch the kindness spread.

Gratitude Check

Name some people you are grateful for: _____
_____
_____

List some places you are grateful for: _____
_____
_____

Write some things you are grateful for: _____
_____
_____

Celebrate You!

You are one of a kind. No, really! In the whole history of the world there has never been anyone exactly like you. Complete this activity to celebrate what makes you unique!

I am really good at:

I am proud of myself for:

Something that makes me stand out is:

Three things that make me special are:

Practice Healthy Self-Talk

You know its unkind to put down a friend or family member, but do you ever catch your inner voice putting yourself down? Review your responses above and create three "I am" statements. For example, if you wrote that you were good at chess, you might say "I am strategic and creative."

I am   I am   I am

These statements are called affirmations! Make colorful posters to showcase your affirmations and hang them somewhere that you'll see them regularly. Repeat your affirmations to yourself whenever you need a reminder of the wonderful things that make you unique.

Kind to My Family

Ways to Be Kind to My Family

Families come in all shapes and sizes, but the one thing they should all have in common is love. If you think of kindness as an expression of love, then who better to be kind to than your own family?! By building a habit of kindness at home, you're contributing to a happy household. Let's explore the many ways you can be kind to your family!

1 Do Your Part at Home.

   ✓ Understand your family's needs.
   ✓ Help out around your home.

2 Extend Grace to Your Family.

   ✓ Practice Patience
   ✓ Go above and beyond.

3 Be Flexible.

   ✓ Go with the flow.
   ✓ Experiment with Different

Complete the blue notepad!

About My Family

Here's who is in my family:

Something we love to do together:

My favorite family tradition:

Doing my Part at Home

Everyone in your family who is old enough should have some responsibilities at home. Whether it's as simple as clearing the table or as big as taking care of a pet, doing your part shows that you're thinking of others. But is there anything else you could do to spread kindness at home? Try these activities to find out!

Family Interview

Pick one member of your family to interview. Write their responses below. To take it further, repeat this interview with every member of your family!

Interview Questions

What is your favorite way to relax?

What do you wish you had more time for?

What is something that you wish your family would remember?

What is your least favorite chore or responsibility?

Pitching In

With the information from your family interview in mind, try some of these ideas to spread kindness at home.

Good for folding the laundry

Make a coupon book that your family member can use whenever they'd like some help with chores.

Work with your grownup to arrange a day for your family member to take a break doing their favorite activity.

Add your family member's least favorite chore to your to-do list once in a while.

Write Your Own Ideas Here

Extending Grace to my Family

What does it mean to extend grace to someone? It means to give them the benefit of the doubt, and to assume everyone is trying their best. Things don't always go the way we'd like, but by extending grace to your family you can make the difficult moments a little easier. Try these small steps to spread big kindness.

Practice Patience

Review the scenarios below and circle the response that extends grace.

1   A parent or caregiver tells you that you cannot watch a show.

   "That's not fair, I'm allowed to watch one show a day!"

   "I feel disappointed, but it seems like you need my help right now. What can I do?"

2   A friend or sibling is insisting that you play what they want to play.

   "It seems like this idea is really important to you. Why don't we do it for a while, and then maybe we can try one of my ideas?"

   "We always do what you want to do!"

3   A family member can no longer take you for ice cream like they promised.

   "But you promised!"

   "You must have a lot going on if you don't have time for ice cream! Let me know if I can do anything to help, and let's find another time to go."

Go Above and Beyond

Going above and beyond means doing more than is expected of you. Between school, home, and activities, kids have a lot of responsibilities. But how would your family feel if you went above and beyond for them once in a while? By doing more than is expected of you, you can extend grace-- and kindness-- to your family. Circle some of the ideas below that you can try at home.

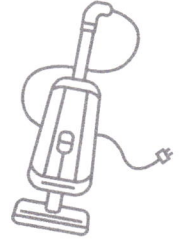

Offer to do someone else's chores one day

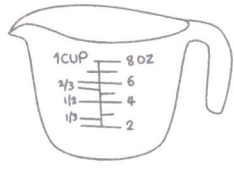

With your grownup's permission, put together a simple dinner for your family

Clean a shared room (like the living room) without being asked

Organize the junk drawer

Offer your family members a drink or a snack

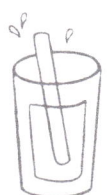

Simply ask your family if there is anything they need help with

Being Flexible with my Family

We know that someone with a flexible body can bend and stretch without getting hurt, and that can be true of someone with a flexible mindset, too! And just like with flexible muscles, you can become more mentally flexible by stretching and practicing every day. Having the skills to switch gears and finding new solutions to problems can help you adapt to all kinds of situations in life! Try this activity to practice flexibility with your family.

Go with the Flow

Read the scenarios below and then choose one. Draw a comic strip that shows how you can approach your scenario with flexibility.

1 Your family is going to the theater to see the movie you've been wanting to see all year. When you arrive, you learn that tickets are sold out.

2 On your family's way to the theme park, you get a flat tire and have to wait in a near by town for hours while it gets fixed. You wont get there before it closes.

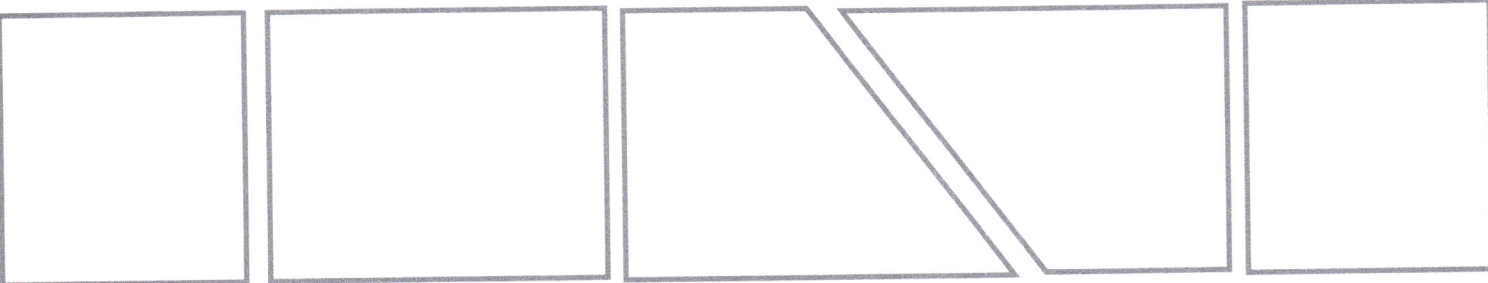

Experiment with Different

Routines, like going to bed at the same time each night, are very important for our wellbeing. But do you ever find yourself doing the same things each day just, well, because? List three small things at home that you could change one day this week, and see what it feels like to have a different day with your family!

Here's some ideas to get you started:

Instead of asking your parent for your regular snack, you could try something new!

Instead of playing the same video game with your sibling, you could do a craft together!

Remember, just because you try something once, doesn't mean you have to do it forever. It can be fun to mix things up!

1 _____

2 _____

3 _____

Kind to My Peers

Ways to Be Kind to My Peers

Your peers include your friends, kids at school, kids in sports and activities, and even kids on the playground who you don't yet know. Outside of your family, your peers are probably the people you spend the most time with, and spreading kindness can not only brighten someone's day—it can inspire them to be kind as well! Let's explore the many ways you can be kind to your peers.

1 Develop Empathy

✓ Be an emotion detective
✓ Put yourself in someone else's shoes

2 Practice Inclusion

✓ Find Common Ground
✓ Explore the power of the invitation

3 Cultivate Belonging

✓ Be yourself
✓ Appreciate diversity

Complete the pink notepad!

About My Peers

Where do you see your peers?

☐ School ☐ Sports/ activities
☐ Clubs ☐ The neighborhood
☐ Other:

What did it feel like when you were the new kid at one of those places?

In which of those places do you feel like you most belong?

Empathy

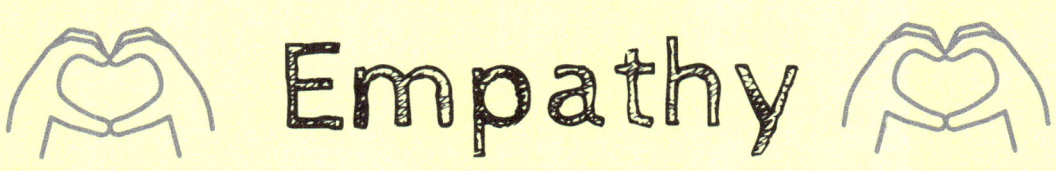

Empathy simply means being able to understand someone else's feelings. How does empathy relate to kindness? By understanding what someone is feeling, you can offer support, lend a helping hand, or just be a good listener. Try these activities to practice empathy with your peers.

Be an Emotion Detective

Become an emotion detective by reading the scenarios and coloring in the emotion you think the person might be feeling.

You're in the cafeteria and a student drops a tray of food, spilling it everywhere. People point and laugh. How might that student be feeling?

You're on the soccer team, and a teammate scores the winning goal.
How might your teammate be feeling?

Your friend tried out for the school play but didn't get the part.
How might your friend be feeling?

26

Put Yourself in Someone Else's Shoes

Have you ever heard the phrase "walk a mile in someone else's shoes"? That means to think about what someone else might have experienced and how they might be feeling. Read the scenario below. In the green shoe print, write how the student is feeling. In the pink shoe print, write what the student experienced and how she behaved.

A new kid on the bus doesn't have anyone to sit with, and is staring out the window with her hood up. She misses her stop and another student teases her. She yells at the other student and storms off the bus.

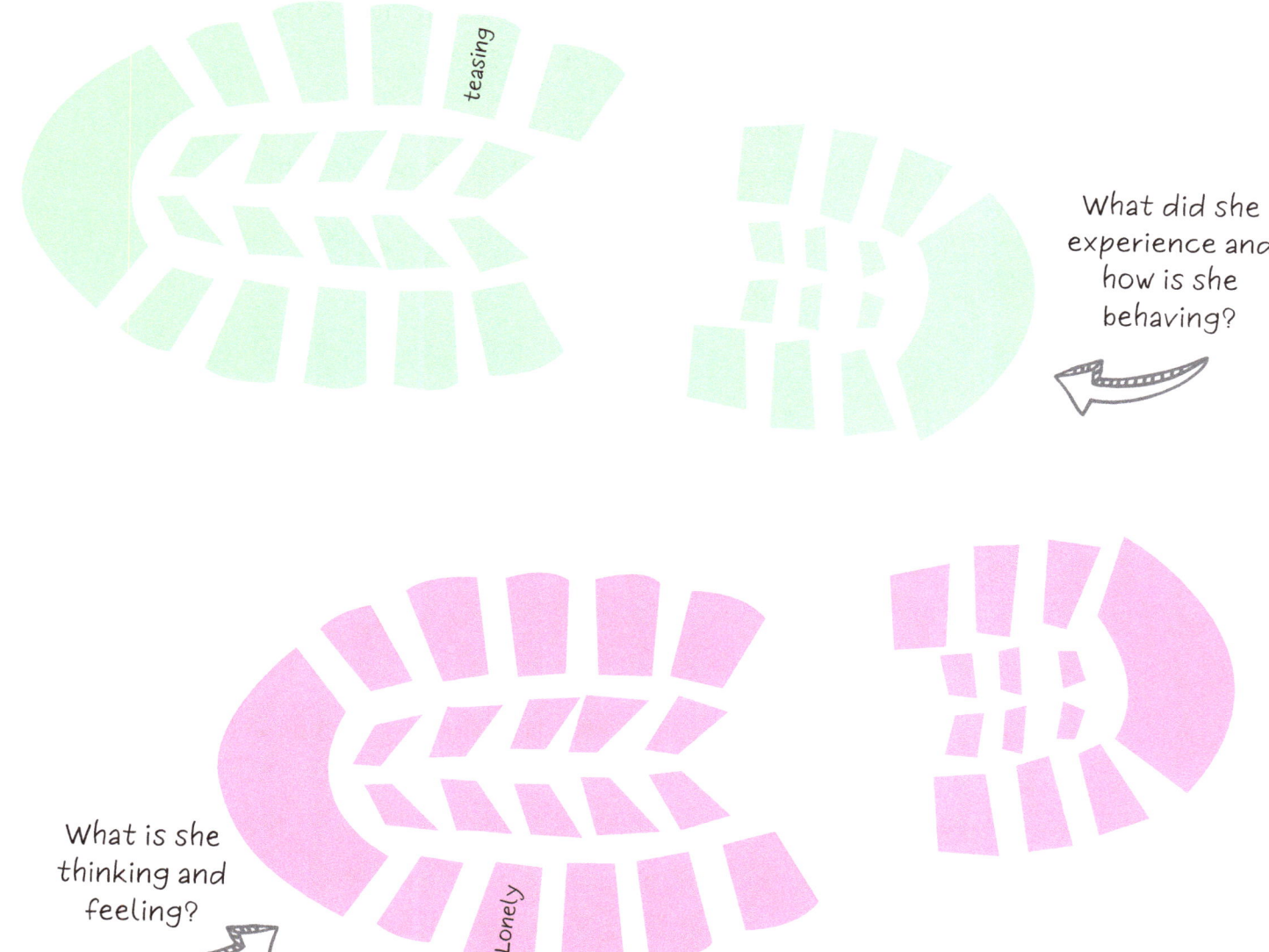

teasing

What did she experience and how is she behaving?

What is she thinking and feeling?

Lonely

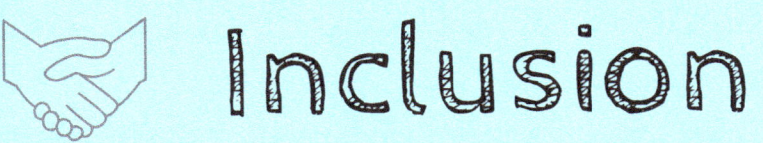

Inclusion

Simply put, inclusion is when someone is made a part of something. Whether having a group to sit with at lunch, or getting invited to a birthday party, developing a habit of inclusion is a powerful act of kindness toward your peers. Try these activities to build a culture of inclusion at school and beyond.

Find Common Ground

Despite all our differences and the things that make us unique, we all have things in common. Finding common ground can help you be inclusive. Make. a list of a few peers in your class, group, or team that you don't know that well yet. Write at least one thing you have in common with each of them. Do you share the same favorite food or have the same type of pet? If you can't think of something, that's a great reason to strike up a conversation!

Name	Commonality

The Power of the Invitation

When you think of an invitation, you might think of asking someone over for a sleepover or inviting them to your birthday party. But there are opportunities for invitations every day! By inviting someone to join you, even in something small, you can spread big kindness!

Match the scenario with the invitation and think about trying some of these yourself!

The teacher asks everyone to find a partner. You end up in a group of three, but notice another student sitting alone.

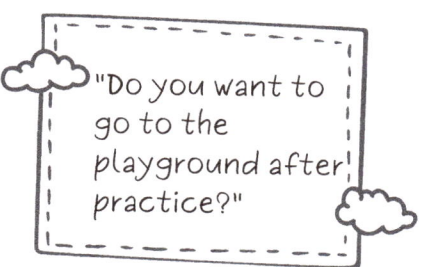

"Do you want to go to the playground after practice?"

You and your friends are playing at recess when you notice some kids sitting out.

"These two can work together and you and I can be partners."

A new kid on your soccer team is shy and is not really talking to anyone.

"Let's see if your neighbor wants to join us."

You're at a friend's house when you learn that a kid from school lives next door.

"Why don't you come and play tag with us?"

Belonging

If inclusion is being invited to join the fun, belonging is when everyone is playing your favorite game when you arrive. Belonging is different from fitting in. Fitting in means trying to be like others in order to be accepted. Belonging means comfortably being yourself, and being accepted for who you are. You can't have belonging without inclusion, and inclusion alone is just the first step. So once you've begun a practice of inclusion, it's time to build a sense of belonging among your peers. Try these activities to get started!

I'll be Myself, you be Yourself

Check out the "celebrate you" and "practice healthy self-talk" activities in the Kind to Myself section of this book. Now, repeat those activities, this time with your peers in mind! Think about a peer or two, and complete the affirmation statements below. Try them out the next time you are together! You can also use these statements to come up with ideas for activities to do together.

You Are   You Are   You Are

Appreciate Diversity

Diversity simply means a group of people or things that are different from one another. Just as we all have things in common, we all have differences. These differences can make us stronger and more creative as a group! Diversity comes in all shapes and sizes, including the things we like to do, our race, ethnicity, gender, disability, age, skills, opinions, beliefs, and so much more. When we appreciate diversity, everyone's unique identity and experience makes the group stronger.

In one band of the rainbow, write your own name. In each of the other five bands of the rainbow, write the names of five peers. Write what makes each of you unique within the corresponding band. In the clouds, write the many things you have in common. Color in your rainbow, and notice how the diversity of colors and words create something more beautiful than any band would be on its own.

Kind to My Community

Ways to Be Kind to My Community

Think of all the places in your community—the library, the grocery store, the park, your school, the fire station, the swimming pool—and how they all contribute to the place you live and learn. When you're kind to your community, you contribute to a positive experience for everyone who lives there or visits. Let's explore the many ways you can spread kindness in your community!

1   Acts of Service

    ✓ Volunteer
    ✓ Raise Awareness & Resources

2   Everyday Practices

    ✓ Lead with Love
    ✓ Be an Ambassador

Complete the green notepad!

About My Community

What kind of community do you live in?

☐ City   ☐ Town
☐ Suburb   ☐ Country

What is your favorite place to visit in your community?

What makes your community special?

 # Acts of Service

Whether serving food to those in need or helping out at the animal shelter, serving others is an impactful way to spread kindness in your community. By doing something to help others, you can spread compassion and love all over town. Ask your grownup to help you explore ways you can serve your community—here are some ideas to get started.

Volunteer

Donating your time can help those in need and non-profit organizations alike. With your grownup's permission, find volunteer opportunities that match your interests and the needs of your community. Volunteering can be as simple as an hour-long event once a year or as big as a weekly commitment. Here are some ideas to get you started.

Read to younger kids at the library

Offer to rake an older neighbor's leaves or shovel their driveway

Sign up to water and weed at the community garden

Help out at the animal shelter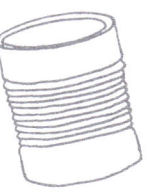

Work a shift at the food pantry

Send thank you notes to first responders

Raise Awareness & Resources

There are probably many organizations dedicated to your community that you are not even aware of. Once you discover them, you can spread kindness by helping them spread the word! Many organizations will also need resources—supplies, materials, and money can help them keep doing the good work. By raising awareness and resources for community organizations, you'll bring kindness to the place you live and learn. Check out these ideas for inspiration.

Organize a can drive to collect food for the food pantry

Rally your community to send care packages to troops

Collect toiletries and assemble care packages for people in need

Make a lemonade stand or bake-sale and donate the proceeds to a local charity

At the holidays, collect toys for kids in need

Put a note about your favorite charity in goodie bags at your birthday party and ask people to get involved

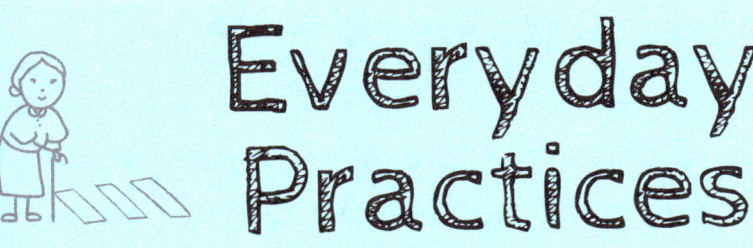

Everyday Practices

While volunteering at events and raising awareness for organizations is a big way to show kindness, the small, kind choices you make every day can add up to make a meaningful difference in your community. By choosing kindness when you're out and about, you're sending a powerful message that your community is a considerate and respectful place. Try some of these ideas the next time you're out!

Lead with Love

Being a leader means that others look to you as an example of how to behave. When you lead with love in your community, you make everyday choices that show you care about the place you call home. Complete this activity to brainstorm ways you can lead with love in your community.

I see a military veteran at the grocery store.
I can _____

The library is having a book sale to raise money.
I can _____

A storm left a lot of damage in a nearby area.
I can _____

A family from another country just moved in.
I can _____

Be an Ambassador

An ambassador is someone who is a positive representative of a group or place. You can become an ambassador for your community by making small acts of kindness your everyday routine. Review these ideas and circle the ones you can try next time you're out in your community.

Hold the door open for someone

Pick up litter

Help a neighbor with yard work

Help a younger child on the playground

Say thank you in stores and restaurants

Ask someone if they need help carrying something

Put your change in the donation or tip jar

Leave positive messages in chalk art

Recycle

Kind to My Planet

REUSE

Ways to Be Kind to My Planet

Think about all the ways the Earth nourishes you and the things you love. From water to drink, to fresh fruit on a summer day, to the air we breathe, everything on our planet works in a delicate balance to support life. But humans have had a big impact on the planet, often in not-so-great ways. It's up to all of us to ensure that the Earth can provide for people, animals, and plants for years to come—by being kind to the planet, you're being kind to everyone and everything on Earth. Let's explore the many ways you can be kind to your planet!

1 Prevention

✓ Live sustainably
✓ Reduce, reuse, recycle

2 Intervention

✓ Clean up your environment
✓ Restore your ecosystem

Complete the blue notepad!

About My Environment

How would you describe your environment?

Which animals can your see in the wild where you live?

What is your favorite outdoor place?

Prevention

Global warming, extreme weather, pollution—these can feel like big problems that are outside of our control. But prevention (or doing something to stop something else from happening in the first place) is a simple mindset we can all employ when being kind to our planet. Try some of these ideas to live every day with kindness toward the Earth.

Live Sustainably

Living sustainably means using fewer of the Earth's resources, which helps keep things in balance. Review these steps toward living sustainably and circle some you can try to start making a difference today.

Try making zero waste one day per week.

Buy things second hand.

Pick one day per week to go meat-free.

Use reusable containers and bottles instead of single-use items.

Turn the water off while brushing your teeth & take shorter showers.

Write your own ideas here:

Reduce, Reuse, Recycle

Reducing what you use, repurposing things you have, and recycling materials to keep them out of the landfill are all parts a sustainable lifestyle. Complete this activity to make living by the three Rs an everyday act of kindness.

Three things I can reduce (or use less of)

1 _____

2 _____

3 _____

Three things I can reuse (or find a new purpose for)

1 _____

2 _____

3 _____

Three things I can recycle (so the materials can be used again)

1 _____

2 _____

3 _____

 # Intervention

The prevention ideas you committed to are so important for the health of the planet, but unfortunately a lot of damage has already been done. Intervention means taking action to make something better, and it can spread big kindness to mother Earth. Explore these ideas to learn how you can step up and make a difference.

Clean Up Your Environment

See that candy wrapper on the sidewalk? See that bottle on the beach? See that balloon tangled in a branch? All this litter has a terrible effect on the environment. Animals can get tangled up in it or eat things that make them sick. And a lot of that garbage ends up in our oceans, with devastating impact on the Earth's largest ecosystem. Cleaning up your environment is one way to be kind to our planet. Check out these ideas and make an action plan!

Bring a garbage bag and collect litter on your walk to the bus or to school

Grab some friends and go to the park to clean up litter

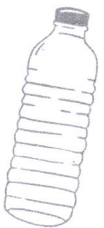 On your next visit to the beach, pack a garbage bag and pick up trash

 Challenge your teammates to a speed round of litter collection after practice

 Join your grownup on their next walk and pick up garbage as you go

Restore Your Ecosystem

Litter isn't the only way humans have harmed the Earth. Pollution from factories can harm insects, pesticides can wipe out important critters and the animals who eat them, and invasive plants and animals can disrupt the balance that all life needs. You can spread kindness to our planet by taking steps to restore your ecosystem, and giving plants and animals a happy oasis to thrive. Complete this activity to help bring harmony back to your own environment.

Research three plants native to your area. Try to find plants that pollinators, like butterflies and bees, need.

Three Plants Native to my Area

1 _____

2 _____

3 _____

Plant a Pollinator Garden!

Now that you know which plants your local pollinators need, plant a pollinator garden! It doesn't matter if you live on a farm or in a city apartment, even a single plant can be a welcome site to a pollinator. Circle which option works best for you. Ask your local community garden how to get seeds or clippings for your garden.

 Container garden  Backyard garden  Field of flowers

Daily Journal

Daily Journal

HOW DID KINDNESS IMPACT YOUR DAY?

WRITE ABOUT KINDNESS YOU SHOWED, OR KINDNESS YOU RECEIVED.

[Date:] _____

_____

_____

_____

_____

WHICH LEVELS OF KINDNESS DID YOU ACHIEVE TODAY?

- ☐ KIND TO MYSELF
- ☐ KIND TO MY FAMILY
- ☐ KIND TO MY PEERS
- ☐ KIND TO MY COMMUNITY
- ☐ KIND TO MY PLANET

WHICH EMOTIONS HAVE YOU FELT TODAY?

HOW WOULD YOU RATE THE DAY?

DRAW A PICTURE OF ONE ACT OF KINDNESS YOU EXPERIENCED TODAY

Daily Journal

HOW DID KINDNESS IMPACT YOUR DAY?

WRITE ABOUT KINDNESS YOU SHOWED, OR KINDNESS YOU RECEIVED.

[Date:] _____

_____

_____

_____

_____

WHICH LEVELS OF KINDNESS DID YOU
ACHIEVE TODAY?

DRAW A PICTURE OF ONE ACT OF
KINDNESS YOU EXPERIENCED TODAY

KIND TO MYSELF

KIND TO MY FAMILY

KIND TO MY PEERS

KIND TO MY COMMUNITY

KIND TO MY PLANET

WHICH EMOTIONS HAVE YOU FELT
TODAY?

HOW WOULD YOU RATE THE DAY?

Daily Journal

HOW DID KINDNESS IMPACT YOUR DAY?

WRITE ABOUT KINDNESS YOU SHOWED, OR KINDNESS YOU RECEIVED.

[Date:]

_____

_____

_____

_____

WHICH LEVELS OF KINDNESS DID YOU ACHIEVE TODAY?

☐ KIND TO MYSELF

☐ KIND TO MY FAMILY

☐ KIND TO MY PEERS

☐ KIND TO MY COMMUNITY

☐ KIND TO MY PLANET

WHICH EMOTIONS HAVE YOU FELT TODAY?

HOW WOULD YOU RATE THE DAY?

DRAW A PICTURE OF ONE ACT OF KINDNESS YOU EXPERIENCED TODAY

Daily Journal

HOW DID KINDNESS IMPACT YOUR DAY?

WRITE ABOUT KINDNESS YOU SHOWED, OR KINDNESS YOU RECEIVED.

[Date:]

_____

_____

_____

_____

WHICH LEVELS OF KINDNESS DID YOU ACHIEVE TODAY?

DRAW A PICTURE OF ONE ACT OF KINDNESS YOU EXPERIENCED TODAY

KIND TO MYSELF

KIND TO MY FAMILY

KIND TO MY PEERS

KIND TO MY COMMUNITY

KIND TO MY PLANET

WHICH EMOTIONS HAVE YOU FELT TODAY?

HOW WOULD YOU RATE THE DAY?

Daily Journal

HOW DID KINDNESS IMPACT YOUR DAY?

WRITE ABOUT KINDNESS YOU SHOWED, OR KINDNESS YOU RECEIVED.

[Date:]

_____

_____

_____

_____

WHICH LEVELS OF KINDNESS DID YOU ACHIEVE TODAY?

- ☐ KIND TO MYSELF
- ☐ KIND TO MY FAMILY
- ☐ KIND TO MY PEERS
- ☐ KIND TO MY COMMUNITY
- ☐ KIND TO MY PLANET

WHICH EMOTIONS HAVE YOU FELT TODAY?

HOW WOULD YOU RATE THE DAY?

DRAW A PICTURE OF ONE ACT OF KINDNESS YOU EXPERIENCED TODAY

Daily Journal

HOW DID KINDNESS IMPACT YOUR DAY?

WRITE ABOUT KINDNESS YOU SHOWED, OR KINDNESS YOU RECEIVED.

[Date:]

_____

_____

_____

_____

WHICH LEVELS OF KINDNESS DID YOU ACHIEVE TODAY?

DRAW A PICTURE OF ONE ACT OF KINDNESS YOU EXPERIENCED TODAY

KIND TO MYSELF

KIND TO MY FAMILY

KIND TO MY PEERS

KIND TO MY COMMUNITY

KIND TO MY PLANET

WHICH EMOTIONS HAVE YOU FELT TODAY?

HOW WOULD YOU RATE THE DAY?

Daily Journal

HOW DID KINDNESS IMPACT YOUR DAY?

WRITE ABOUT KINDNESS YOU SHOWED, OR KINDNESS YOU RECEIVED.

[Date:]

_____

_____

_____

_____

WHICH LEVELS OF KINDNESS DID YOU ACHIEVE TODAY?

- [ ] KIND TO MYSELF
- [ ] KIND TO MY FAMILY
- [ ] KIND TO MY PEERS
- [ ] KIND TO MY COMMUNITY
- [ ] KIND TO MY PLANET

WHICH EMOTIONS HAVE YOU FELT TODAY?

HOW WOULD YOU RATE THE DAY?

DRAW A PICTURE OF ONE ACT OF KINDNESS YOU EXPERIENCED TODAY

Weekly Tracker

Date:

Weekly Kindness Tracker

ADD THE NAMES OF WHO YOU WERE KIND TOWARD AND CHECK THE DAY
OF THE WEEK THAT IT HAPPENED.

AIM FOR AT LEAST ONE CHECKMARK EVERY DAY!

Who Were you Kind to?	M	T	W	TH	F	S	SU
_____	○	○	○	○	○	○	○
_____	○	○	○	○	○	○	○
_____	○	○	○	○	○	○	○
_____	○	○	○	○	○	○	○
_____	○	○	○	○	○	○	○
_____	○	○	○	○	○	○	○
_____	○	○	○	○	○	○	○

Draw your favorite moment of kindness from the week!

Date:

Weekly Kindness Tracker

ADD THE NAMES OF WHO YOU WERE KIND TOWARD AND CHECK THE DAY OF THE WEEK THAT IT HAPPENED.

AIM FOR AT LEAST ONE CHECKMARK EVERY DAY!

Who Were you Kind to?	M	T	W	TH	F	S	SU
_____							
_____							
_____							
_____							
_____							
_____							

Draw your favorite moment of kindness from the week!

Date: Weekly Kindness Tracker

ADD THE NAMES OF WHO YOU WERE KIND TOWARD AND CHECK THE DAY
OF THE WEEK THAT IT HAPPENED.

AIM FOR AT LEAST ONE CHECKMARK EVERY DAY!

Who Were you Kind to?	M	T	W	TH	F	S	SU
_____							
_____							
_____							
_____							
_____							
_____							
_____							

Draw your favorite moment of kindness from the week!

Date:

Weekly Kindness Tracker

ADD THE NAMES OF WHO YOU WERE KIND TOWARD AND CHECK THE DAY
OF THE WEEK THAT IT HAPPENED.

AIM FOR AT LEAST ONE CHECKMARK EVERY DAY!

Who Were you Kind to?	M	T	W	TH	F	S	SU
_____							
_____							
_____							
_____							
_____							
_____							
_____							

Draw your favorite moment of kindness from the week!

Monthly Tracker

January

Every day, check off each kindness category you achieved.

1 2 3 4 5 6 7

8 9 10 11 12 13 14

15 16 17 18 19 20 21

22 23 24 25 26 27 28

29 30 31

Self
Family
Peers
Community
Planet

58

February

Every day, check off each kindness category you achieved.

1 2 3 4 5 6 7

8 9 10 11 12 13 14

15 16 17 18 19 20 21

22 23 24 25 26 27 28

29

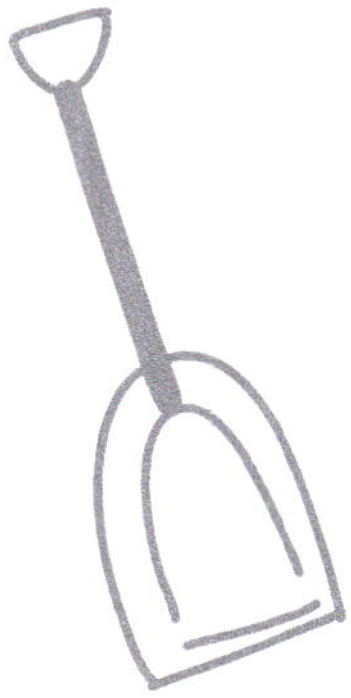

Self
Family
Peers
Community
Planet

March

Every day, check off each kindness category you achieved.

1   2   3   4   5   6   7

8   9   10   11   12   13   14

15   16   17   18   19   20   21

22   23   24   25   26   27   28

29   30   31

Self
Family
Peers
Community
Planet

April

Every day, check off each kindness category you achieved.

1	2	3	4	5	6	7
8	9	10	11	12	13	14
15	16	17	18	19	20	21
22	23	24	25	26	27	28
29	30					

Self
Family
Peers
Community
Planet

May

Every day, check off each kindness category you achieved.

1	2	3	4	5	6	7
8	9	10	11	12	13	14
15	16	17	18	19	20	21
22	23	24	25	26	27	28
29	30	31				

Self
Family
Peers
Community
Planet

June

Every day, check off each kindness category you achieved.

| 1 | 2 | 3 | 4 | 5 | 6 | 7 |

| 8 | 9 | 10 | 11 | 12 | 13 | 14 |

| 15 | 16 | 17 | 18 | 19 | 20 | 21 |

| 22 | 23 | 24 | 25 | 26 | 27 | 28 |

| 29 | 30 |

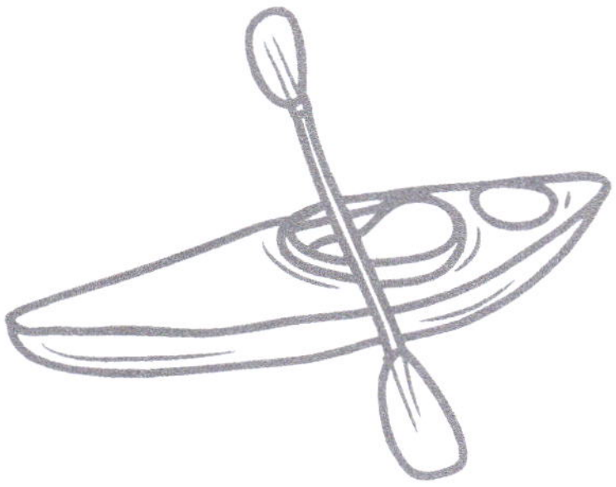

- Self
- Family
- Peers
- Community
- Planet

July

Every day, check off each kindness category you achieved.

1 2 3 4 5 6 7

8 9 10 11 12 13 14

15 16 17 18 19 20 21

22 23 24 25 26 27 28

29 30 31

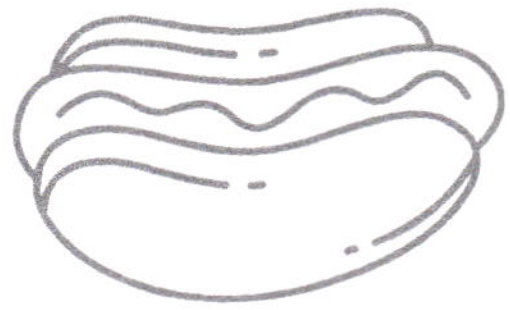

Self
Family
Peers
Community
Planet

64

August

Every day, check off each kindness category you achieved.

1   2   3   4   5   6   7

8   9   10   11   12   13   14

15   16   17   18   19   20   21

22   23   24   25   26   27   28

29   30   31

- Self
- Family
- Peers
- Community
- Planet

65

September

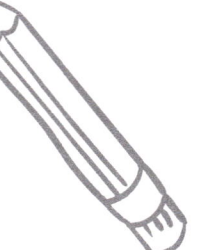

Every day, check off each kindness category you achieved.

1   2   3   4   5   6   7

8   9   10   11   12   13   14

15   16   17   18   19   20   21

22   23   24   25   26   27   28

29   30

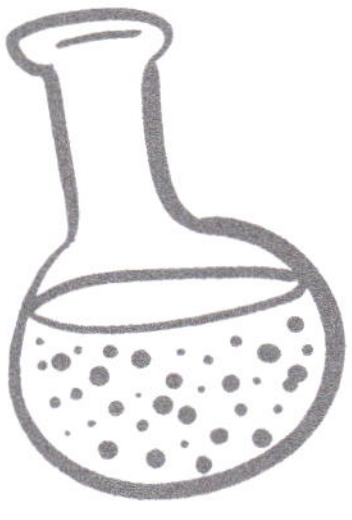

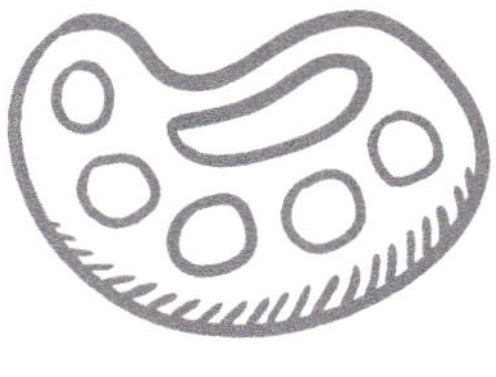

Self (yellow)
Family (light blue)
Peers (yellow)
Community (pink)
Planet (teal)

October

Every day, check off each kindness category you achieved.

1 2 3 4 5 6 7

8 9 10 11 12 13 14

15 16 17 18 19 20 21

22 23 24 25 26 27 28

29 30 31

	Self
	Family
	Peers
	Community
	Planet

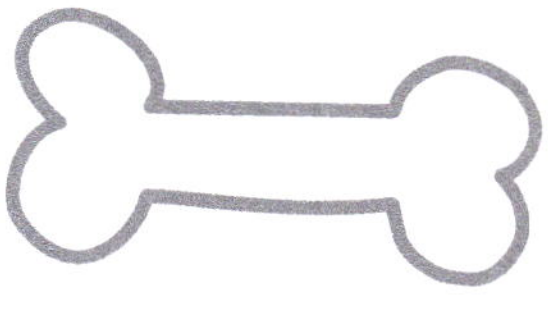

67

November

Every day, check off each kindness category you achieved.

1 2 3 4 5 6 7

8 9 10 11 12 13 14

15 16 17 18 19 20 21

22 23 24 25 26 27 28

29 30 31

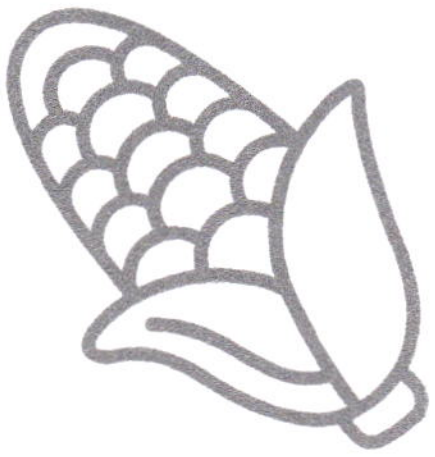

🟡	Self
⚪	Family
🟡	Peers
🩷	Community
🩵	Planet

68

December

Every day, check off each kindness category you achieved.

1 2 3 4 5 6 7

8 9 10 11 12 13 14

15 16 17 18 19 20 21

22 23 24 25 26 27 28

29 30 31

Self
Family
Peers
Community
Planet

69

Certificate of Kindness

I pledge to be:

Kind to myself

Kind to my family

Kind to my peers

Kind to my community

Kind to my planet

Name:

Date: